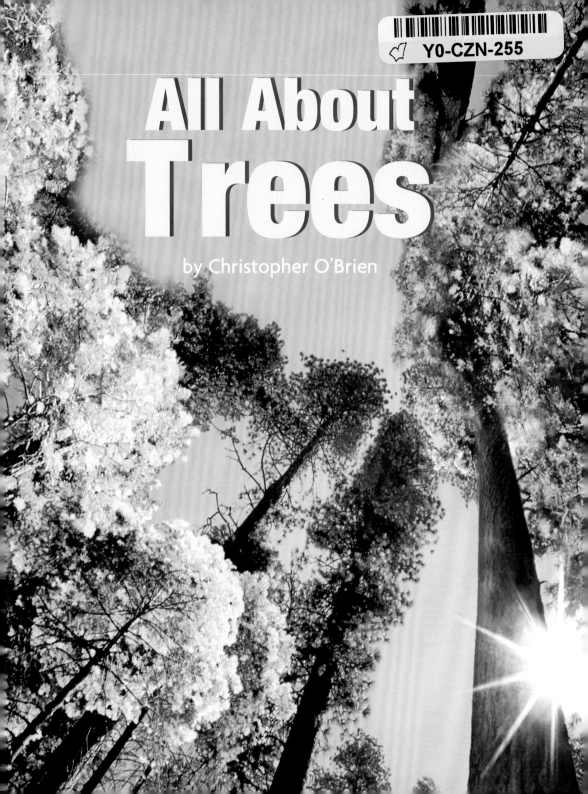

# All About Trees

by Christopher O'Brien

# I need to know these words.

bark

branches

buds

2

**leaves**

**roots**

**tree**

3

Do you like fruit? Some fruit grows on this tree.

  ▲ These apples grow on this tree.

Do you like nuts? Some nuts grow on this tree.

▲ This tree has nuts.

How are the trees alike? Both trees have the same parts.

buds

branches

leaves

▲ Both trees have these parts.

What are the parts of a tree?
A tree has roots. The roots grow
into the ground. The roots keep
the tree in place.

roots

▲ The roots can grow very long.

A tree also has a trunk.
The trunk grows above
the ground.

▲ Some animals live inside a tree trunk.

The trunk has bark on
the outside. The bark is hard.

bark

▲ The bark protects the trunk.

A tree has branches.
Some branches are thick.
Some branches are thin.

▲ A tree can have many branches.

Some trees have branches that point up. Some trees have branches that spread out.

◀ These branches point up.

These branches spread out.

The branches grow leaves.
The leaves start as buds. Do
you see the buds on this branch?

buds

▲ These buds are on a tree
that grows apples.

You can see flowers on branches, too. Some flowers turn into fruit. Some flowers turn into nuts.

▲ The nut started as a flower. The apples started as flowers, too. ▶

All trees make food.
The leaves help make the food.

▲ These leaves help make food for this tree.

Have you ever looked closely at leaves? Leaves can be many shapes.

▲ These leaves are different shapes.

People can eat some parts of a tree. People can eat apples. People can eat nuts, too.